S0-BAW-363

Livonia Public Library
ALFRED NOBLE BRANCH
32901 PLYMOUTH ROAD
Livonia, Michigan 48150-1793
421-6600
LIVN #19

J973.927
G

RSVP

RAINTREE
STECK-VAUGHN
P U B L I S H E R S
A Steck-Vaughn Company

Austin, Texas
www.steck-vaughn.com

A LOOK AT LIFE IN

The Eighties

Adrian Gilbert

Livonia Public Library
ALFRED NOBLE BRANCH
32901 PLYMOUTH ROAD
Livonia, Michigan 48150-1793
421-6600
LIVN #19

© Copyright 2000, text, Steck-Vaughn Company

All rights reserved. No part of this book may be reproduced or utilized in any form or by any means, electronic or mechanical, including photocopying, recording, or by any information storage and retrieval system, without permission in writing from the Publisher. Inquiries should be addressed to: Copyright Permissions, Steck-Vaughn Company, P.O. Box 26015, Austin, TX 78755.

Published by Raintree Steck-Vaughn Publishers, an imprint of Steck-Vaughn Company

Printed in Italy. Bound in the United States.
1 2 3 4 5 6 7 8 9 0 04 03 02 01 00

Library of Congress Cataloging-in-Publication Data

Gilbert, Adrian.
The eighties / Adrian Gilbert.
    p.   cm.—(A look at life)
    Includes bibliographical references and index.
    Summary: Traces the events, trends, and important people of the 1980s, including science, technology, fashion, music, art, architecture, sports, entertainment, and news.
    ISBN 0-7398-1341-2
    1. Civilization, Modern, --1950—Juvenile literature.
    2. Nineteen eighties—Juvenile literature.
    [1. Nineteen eighties. 2. United States—History—1969. 3. United States—Social life and customs—1971-]
    I. Title. II. Series.
    CB429.G55   2000
    909.82'8—dc21   99-39797

JUL 0 7 2005

Cover photographs

Top left: Mikhail Gorbachev and Ronald Reagan in Red Square, Moscow, May 1988 (Topham Picturepoint)

Top right: Arnold Schwarzenegger in *The Terminator* (Orion, courtesy Kobal)

Center: The space shuttle *Discovery* heads for Earth orbit, September 1988 (Popperfoto)

Bottom left: The Louvre pyramid, Paris (Topham Picturepoint)

Bottom right: Madonna, 1987 (Topham Picturepoint)

Acknowledgments

The Author and Publishers thank the following for their permission to reproduce photographs: Camera Press: pages 4b, 5b, 6, 7t, 7b, 10b, 11t, 11b, 12b, 14–15b, 16t, 18b, 19, 20t, 22t, 22b, 23b, 25t, 26, 27t, 27b, 28–29t, 29b, 30b, 31t, 31b, 34b, 37b, 39, 40t, 40b; Robert Harding Picture Library: pages 12t, 14t, 18t; Popperfoto: pages 8, 9t, 9b, 10t, 25b, 32, 33t, 33b, 34t, 35t, 35b; Retna Pictures: pages 21, 23t, 24; Science Photo Library: pages 4–5t (Alex Bartel), 13 (Phillip Hayson), 15t (Joyce Photographics); Spelling/ABC (courtesy Kobal): page 36b; Topham Picturepoint: pages 16b, 28b, 30t, 36–37t; Touchstone/Amblin (courtesy Kobal): page 38b; Universal (courtesy Kobal): page 38t. Page 17: © The Estate of Keith Haring

3 9082 09670 7867

Contents

A Look at...

...in the '80s

A LOOK AT
THE NEWS
IN THE '80s

▷ *New technology enabled stock exchanges around the world to share information instantly.*

The 1980s was a time when making money and enjoying material prosperity were thought to be very important. Governments encouraged free enterprise: businesspeople (sometimes called entrepreneurs) were free to make money for themselves by providing goods and services to others.

Reagan and Thatcher

Ronald Reagan became president of the United States in 1981. As well as encouraging free enterprise, he tried to reduce the amount of money spent by the government so that people could pay lower taxes.

❝ ❞

Margaret Thatcher explained, half jokingly, how she ran her government:

"I don't mind how much my ministers talk, as long as they do what I say."

As president, Reagan found a friend and ally in the British prime minister, Margaret Thatcher. She was a very strong-minded person, admired by some people, but bitterly disliked by others. Like Reagan, she wanted to reduce the role that government played in people's lives. Both leaders believed that individuals should be free to make their own decisions about jobs and money, rather than being told what to do by the government.

Money markets

The financial world received greater attention in the 1980s. Many of the old laws that had

▽ *President Reagan (left) and Margaret Thatcher were among the representatives to a United Nations conference held in Cancun, Mexico, in 1981. (See page 46 for a list of everyone in the picture.)*

controlled stock markets and banks were removed in what became known as deregulation. At the same time, new computerized electronic trading systems were introduced, which enabled stockbrokers to buy and sell shares without delay. These developments led to an international financial system, where enterprising individuals could make (and lose) fortunes within minutes just by trading shares.

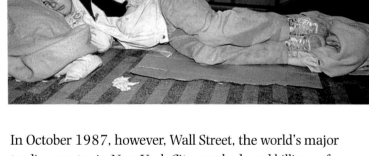

▷ *During the 1980s many people became homeless and were forced to live on city streets.*

...Newsflash...

Washington D.C., March 30, 1981. President Ronald Reagan was shot in the chest today as he walked to his car. Two of his aides were also wounded when John W. Hinckley fired a hail of shots. Reagan was rushed to the George Washington University Hospital, where he underwent two hours of surgery. His doctors expect him to make a full recovery. He quipped to his wife, Nancy: "Honey, I forgot to duck." The motives for the assassination attempt are unknown. Hinckley will undergo psychiatric testing before facing trial.

In October 1987, however, Wall Street, the world's major trading center in New York City, crashed, and billions of dollars were lost in a single day. This caused problems around the world, affecting the economies of many countries. The 1987 crash was the start of a recession, which meant that unemployment increased and people had less to spend.

Many of the unemployed came from the old manufacturing and mining industries such as coal, steel, and shipbuilding. It was very hard for them to find new jobs. This caused great distress, not only to the unemployed and their families, but to the communities in which they lived.

Cold warriors
Reagan and Thatcher were both strongly opposed to communism, and during the 1980s they encouraged opposition to communist regimes, especially the Soviet Union. The United States increased the size of its armed forces and began the SDI (Strategic Defense Initiative), or "Star Wars"

program. The idea was to build rockets and lasers capable of shooting down Soviet missiles while they were still in space. Although the SDI was eventually abandoned, it was an example of how the Cold War (the rivalry between communist states and those of the Western world) got worse in the 1980s.

At the end of 1979, the Soviet Union had invaded Afghanistan to prevent the communist Afghan government from being taken over by local Islamic rebels. Many Western governments decided to support the rebels.

△ *Afghan rebels, known as mujahidin (holy warriors)*

...Newsflash...

Grenada, November 6, 1983. The tiny Caribbean island of Grenada has come under American control. U.S. troops invaded the island on October 31, to get rid of the new communist government of Bernard Coard. Although supported by Cuban military advisers, Coard's forces were unable to repel the attack. President Reagan says that he needed to protect the thousand Americans living in Grenada, but it is probable that he wishes to give other nations in Central America the message that he will not tolerate communist regimes so close to the United States.

They sent arms and equipment to aid the rebels in their fight against the Soviet Army. The war lasted until the Soviets withdrew in 1988, but fighting in Afghanistan between rival rebel groups continued well into the 1990s.

In Central America and the Caribbean, the United States aided groups or governments fighting against socialists and communists. In El Salvador, the United States financed the right-wing government in its war against left-wing (socialist) rebels. Despite a Congressional ban, the Reagan administration illegally gave arms and money to the Contras. The Contras fought the socialist but democratically elected government of Nicaragua. Some of the aid to the Contras came from the administration's sale of arms to Iran. This, too, was illegal, and President Reagan received sharp criticism and suffered a decline in popularity because of these actions.

Global wars

There were many wars, fought all around the world, during the 1980s. Argentina invaded the Falkland Islands in 1982. Though close to Argentina, the islands were British. After several pitched battles, the Argentinians were forced to surrender and return the Falklands to British control.

In 1982, Israel's army entered Lebanon, a country from which Palestinian terrorists of the PLO (Palestine Liberation Organization) made attacks on Israel. The Palestinians fought the invading Israelis, and both sides suffered heavy casualties. Eventually, the better armed Israelis forced the PLO out of Lebanon, but many towns and cities were destroyed, including much of the Lebanese capital of Beirut.

▷ *Muslim women in Lebanon march behind a portrait of Ayatollah Khomeini, who ruled in Iran.*

▽ *Fighting in Lebanon left the capital, Beirut, severely damaged.*

Islamic fundamentalism

The Israeli invasion of the predominantly Arab state of Lebanon caused great anger throughout the Islamic world. The 1980s was a time when many people of the Islamic faith became increasingly angry at what they saw as the injustices suffered by their people. This anger was combined with the growth of Islamic fundamentalism, a movement that believed in the strict observance of the Islamic faith.

Hardline fundamentalist groups used violence to promote their aims and even attacked the governments of their own countries if they thought they were not religious enough. But, above all, Islamic fundamentalists were opposed to the state of Israel and those nations in the West who supported Israel.

After the overthrow of the Shah (or king) in 1979, Iran was governed by extremist Islamic religious leaders under the overall rule of Ayatollah Khomeini. Iran now became a center for extreme anti-Western views. Although Iran was engaged in a brutal war with its neighbor Iraq, it still found time and resources to support terrorists fighting Israel and the West.

...Newsflash...

Washington, May 18, 1980. Mount St. Helens, the fifth-highest mountain in the state, erupted this morning. The volcano, located in the Cascade Mountains, sent hot clouds of ash rolling down its sides. The clouds reached a temperature of 500° F (260° C), and burned hundreds of trees in its wake. Sixty-six people are feared dead as a result of the eruption. In the past few weeks, seismologists had noticed minor tremors in the area. A part of Mount St. Helens' summit had recently been bulging outward until just before the eruption.

Hijacking and hostage-taking

The hijacking or destruction of passenger aircraft had become a common form of terrorism during the 1970s, and this continued into the 1980s. In 1985, an Iranian-backed Lebanese group hijacked a TWA plane flying from Athens to Rome. The group took 39 hostages to a hideout in Beirut and later managed to exchange them for 735 Islamic fundamentalists held in Israeli prisons.

Not all attacks on aircraft were made by Islamic groups, however. A Korean 747 jetliner was shot down by Soviet fighters in 1983, killing 269 passengers.

" "

The pilot of the hijacked TWA flight radioed to his flight controllers:

"They are beating up the passengers. We must land in Beirut. He has pulled a hand-grenade pin and is ready to blow up the aircraft ..."

Another type of terrorism was the kidnapping of foreigners working in Lebanon. During the 1980s, 23 people—Americans, Indians, Saudi Arabians, and Europeans—were taken hostage by the Iranian-backed Hezbollah (Party of God). The hostages were held in very bad conditions and were harshly treated by their captors. Several of them died in captivity. But toward the end of the decade, the survivors slowly began to be released.

◁ *Terry Waite (left), adviser to the Archbishop of Canterbury, went to Lebanon to negotiate the release of hostages. Fourteen were freed in 1982–86, as a result of his work. He was taken hostage himself in 1987 and was freed only in 1991.*

Profile

Cory Aquino (1933–)

The wife of a Philippines politician, Corazon (Cory) Aquino entered politics when her husband was assassinated in 1983. They both opposed the corrupt dictator Ferdinand Marcos. In 1986, after a rigged election, pressure from the people of the Philippines forced Marcos to flee the country, and Cory Aquino became president. She faced many problems as the new leader, but she brought real democracy to her country. In 1992, she decided not to enter the new elections and retired from politics.

Democratic progress

Although most people who lived in Europe and the United States enjoyed democratic government, having a real say in how their countries were run, other people around the world were not so lucky. But some progress toward democracy was made in the 1980s. The people of the Philippines overthrew the corrupt government of Ferdinand Marcos in 1986. The leader of the peaceful revolution, Cory Aquino, freed political prisoners and restored democratic institutions, such as free speech and regular elections.

In Spain, the democratic government faced a great challenge in 1981, when a gang of right-wing army officers took over the Spanish parliament by force, in a plot to overthrow the government. The rest of the army backed the government, however, and King Juan Carlos went on television to denounce the plotters. Supported by the Spanish people, the army units loyal to the government surrounded the plotters, who were then forced to surrender.

▽ *Army officers storm into the Spanish parliament, Madrid, February 2, 1981.*

▷ *Tiananmen Square, Beijing, June 1989: defying the tanks sent in to end demonstrations for reform*

Other advances for democracy took place in South America, where free elections were held in Chile, Argentina, and Brazil, countries that had previously been under the control of the armed forces. In China, however, the democratic movement failed in 1989, when tanks of the Chinese Army crushed a revolt by students in Beijing's Tiananmen Square.

The troubles continue

In Northern Ireland, Catholic republican groups attempted to get rid of the British presence, and the situation continued to be violent. Hunger strikes by republican prisoners were followed by assassinations and bombings. The only ray of hope in this confrontation came in 1985, when the governments of Great Britain and the Irish Republic made an agreement to work together on Northern Irish affairs.

Communism in crisis

The most important news story of the decade was Eastern Europe's gradual turn away from communism. In 1980, Polish trade unionists formed the Solidarity group to oppose their

Profile — Mikhail Gorbachev (1931–)

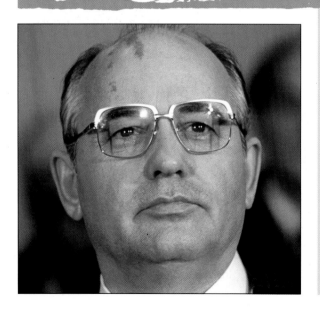

When he became leader of the Soviet Union in 1985, Mikhail Gorbachev began to reform the communist system. He developed the policies of *glasnost* (openness) and *perestroika* (rebuilding), and he tried to make the economy more efficient. Gorbachev called for friendship between the communist countries and the West, and he played a leading role in getting both sides to reduce nuclear weapons. But toward the end of the 1980s, growing economic problems within the Soviet Union made him less popular with the people.

▷ *In Poland, Lech Walesa (right) led the out-lawed Solidarity movement throughout the '80s. In 1989 he was elected president of the country.*

communist government, but they had limited success. The real change was made by Mikhail Gorbachev, who came to power in the Soviet Union in 1985. He relaxed censorship, withdrew Soviet troops from Afghanistan, and loosened the control of the government. His reforms in the Soviet Union encouraged people in communist-dominated Eastern Europe to get rid of their rulers.

The end of communism in much of Eastern Europe happened incredibly quickly in the second half of 1989. In June, elections were held in Poland, and the communists were replaced by the new Solidarity party. On November 10, the Berlin Wall, which divided communist East Berlin from West Berlin, was torn down. This was the first stage of the reunification of East and West Germany.

▽ *East German soldiers break through the Berlin Wall, 1989.*

❝ ❞

West Germany's chancellor, Helmut Kohl, welcomed the destruction of the Berlin Wall by the people of East Germany:

"We're on your side; we are and remain one nation. We belong together."

On November 21, the Czech Communist Party accepted opposition demands to hold multi-party elections. Democratic reforms were announced in both Bulgaria and Yugoslavia on December 15, and on December 17 the overthrow of the communist regime began in Romania.

A LOOK AT
SCIENCE and TECHNOLOGY
IN THE '80s

The speed of change in the world of science and technology seemed to get faster than ever. There were advances in the field of computers and electronics, and in space travel. But damage to the environment continued to be a problem and, despite the best efforts of many scientists, there were major disasters that caused widespread pollution.

The first ever PCs (personal computers) had been invented in the 1970s, but they were expensive and too complex for anyone but a computer expert to use. The great breakthrough in PC development came in 1981, when the U.S. manufacturer IBM (International Business Machines) introduced its personal computer.

△ Electric typewriters were put aside in favor of PCs, which could be used for word processing.

The key to the importance of the IBM PC lay in its software. It used a new operating system developed by the Microsoft Corporation in 1977, called MS-DOS (Microsoft Disc Operating System), which was much easier to use than the older systems. The IBM PC also used the

Profile

Bill Gates (1955–)

One of the first people to understand that computers would become a major part of everybody's life was Bill Gates. He made a fortune by developing software programs with his Microsoft Corporation, a company he set up in Seattle, in 1977. His big break came in the early 1980s, when IBM introduced its Personal Computer (PC). IBM gave a license to Microsoft to develop software that would enable noncomputer specialists to use the new PCs. Soon a Microsoft operating system was being used in virtually every computer sold around the world.

latest, highly advanced silicon chips developed by the Intel Corporation, which enabled the computers to be small yet powerful. The IBM PC helped transform the computer world because it allowed ordinary people to use computers for the first time.

Computers worldwide

The new IBM PC became a great success. In 1981, 25,000 machines were sold; just three years later, the figure had soared to three million. During the 1980s other computer manufacturers began to develop similar machines—called "clones"—and soon PCs were being used worldwide. At first, their main use was in the office, but by the end of the decade PCs were also being used in the home. They proved very popular with children, who used them for educational purposes and to play computer games.

66 99

Bruce Sterling wrote in 1986:

"Eighties tech sticks to the skin, responds to the touch: the personal computer, the portable telephone, the soft contact lens."

The miniaturization of computer components was not used only in PCs. Microcomputers were used in all sorts of modern machines, such as cars, washing machines, telephones— even toasters!

Good-bye
telexes

Hello
Compact discs;
CD-ROMs;
walkmen;
mobile phones;
camcorders;
TV satellite dishes

A revolution in communications

The 1980s computer explosion was part of a greater revolution in the communication of information. Telephone systems provided new opportunities to transmit data. Although fax (short for "facsimile") machines had been introduced in the 1970s, it was not until 1980 that they became an effective means of communication by using ordinary telephone lines. By the mid-1980s even the smallest companies had a fax machine as part of their basic office equipment. And soon fax machines were used in many homes, allowing people to send each other documents at the press of a button.

Another 1980s development using telephone lines to communicate information was the modem. This simple device linked computers to each other, so they could relay messages and documents. The modem was the first step toward the linking up of computers into the World Wide Web and the Internet.

▷ *Fiber-optic cables replaced old telephone wires. Optical fibers are thin, flexible glass tubes. Telephone conversations, images, and computer data are converted into laser signals and sent through the fibers.*

Environmental issues

Although scientists and people working in the field of technology made many great advances, they were unable to solve the old problems of pollution. Efforts were made to make industry more "clean and green," but environmental problems remained serious.

Acid rain became an international political issue in 1982, when Canada accused the United States of causing environmental damage. Acid rain is produced when gases in exhaust fumes from burning fuel react with water in the air to form acids. When the rain falls, it causes harm to plants and animals. The Canadians said that acid rain had drifted northward from the industrial areas of the United States and had fallen on Canadian lakes and rivers, killing large numbers of fish.

◁ Trees in Czechoslovakia damaged by acid rain

Acid rain was also a major problem in Europe during the 1970s and 1980s, especially in parts of West Germany and Scandinavia. The European nations acted quickly to reduce emissions of the most harmful gases, making acid rain less damaging. But the United States was slow to do anything to solve this problem.

New political parties giving top priority to environmental issues gained support in the 1980s. David Icke, spokesman for the Green Party in the UK, said:

"Green politics is not about being far left or far right, but about being far-sighted."

A hole in the sky

In 1985 scientists confirmed the existence of a hole in the ozone layer of the earth's atmosphere. The ozone layer normally reflects harmful ultraviolet rays from the sun. A hole in it allows this radiation to reach the earth. The scientists explained that the hole in the air, high above the South Pole in Antarctica, had been caused by chemicals called CFCs, which were used in aerosol spray cans, refrigerators, and air-conditioning units.

It was found that CFCs also contributed to the "greenhouse effect," which was causing the world to slowly get hotter (also

...Newsflash...

Auckland, New Zealand, July 23, 1985. More information has been revealed about the mysterious sinking of the Greenpeace ship *Rainbow Warrior* on July 10, 1985. The French secret service was behind the explosion that sank the ship at its moorings in Auckland Harbor, killing a freelance photographer. The ship had been used by the environmental organization Greenpeace to protest against France's nuclear testing on remote Pacific islands.

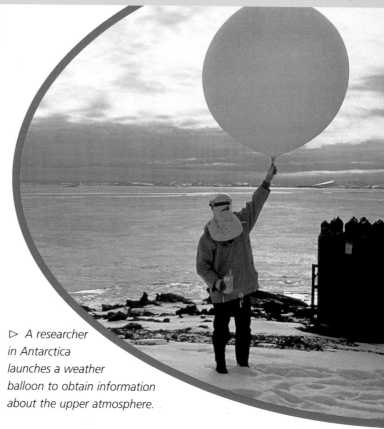

▷ *A researcher in Antarctica launches a weather balloon to obtain information about the upper atmosphere.*

called "global warming"). In response to scientists' warnings about the dangers, 53 industrial countries signed the Montreal Accords in 1987—an agreement to stop using CFCs by 2000.

Global disasters

An accidental leak of poisonous gases from the Bhopal chemical plant in India, on December 3, 1984, killed 2,000 people almost immediately and left 200,000 sick or injured. It was the worst ever industrial disaster. The plant made pesticides, designed to kill insects eating crops, but the disaster showed that technology could be dangerous, hurting the very people it was trying to help.

In April 1986, a major disaster occurred at a nuclear power plant near the Ukrainian city of Chernobyl in the Soviet Union. A full-scale nuclear meltdown took place, and fires burned for two weeks, allowing radioactive material to escape into the atmosphere.

◁ *Scientists check radiation levels in fields around Chernobyl, 1986.*

What made the Chernobyl disaster so serious was that radioactive material was carried around the world in the atmosphere. Many crops in Europe were affected and had to be destroyed. In Scandinavia, milk was found to have 15 times the normal radiation level.

The meltdown occurred because of the reactor's poor design and a lack of proper safety measures. People around the world began to worry that their own nuclear reactors might not be as safe as they had thought.

▽ A space shuttle is launched, 1983. Sometimes shuttles carry scientific experiments. Sometimes they carry satellites to launch into space or take the astronauts to satellites that need repairing.

▷ Three of Saturn's moons, discovered by Voyager 2, can be seen on the left of this picture.

Final frontiers

Space exploration captured the public's imagination during the 1980s. America's two unmanned Voyager probes began to send back superb pictures of the planets in our solar system. Although launched in 1977, it was not until August 1981 that *Voyager 2* reached Saturn, where it discovered eight moons that had been too small to see from Earth.

The United States launched its first space shuttle, named *Columbia*, in 1981. The space shuttle was the first reusable spacecraft. It was launched like a rocket, but it flew like an aircraft; once it had completed a mission, it glided back through the atmosphere to Earth. The *Columbia* mission was a success, but the explosion of the *Challenger* shuttle in 1986 ended in tragedy. Despite this setback, the United States continued to use space shuttles to send men and women into space.

Medical advances and setbacks

The world's first mechanical heart was successfully used in 1982 as a means of keeping a patient alive for a long period until a donor heart was found. Keyhole surgery—a new way of operating on people—also became widespread. The surgeon needed to make only a small cut into the patient's body, and then, using miniaturized surgical instruments, performed the operation by looking through a camera lens inside the patient's body.

In 1980 the World Health Organization announced that the killer disease smallpox had been eradicated. Smallpox had been one of the world's most deadly diseases. Previously, two million people had been killed by smallpox every year.

Unfortunately, the success of the medical profession in getting rid of smallpox was countered a year later by the announcement, on June 5, 1981, of the existence of a new disease called AIDS (Acquired Immune Deficiency Syndrome). Although scientists were not sure how the disease originated, it was transmitted through blood and other bodily fluids. AIDS was a killer disease that soon spread throughout the world, with a number of African countries being particularly hard hit. By the early 1990s, an estimated three million people had contracted AIDS.

People who had AIDS were often shunned. As one AIDS sufferer explained:

"I have a terrible feeling that I am dying not from the virus, but from being untouchable."

▽ *This poster for an AIDS hotline was designed by artist Keith Haring.*

...Newsflash...

Cape Canaveral, Florida, January 28, 1986. After 73 seconds of what seemed a routine launch, the space shuttle *Challenger* suddenly exploded in midair. Watched by millions of stunned people across the globe, the explosion killed all seven crew members instantly. Among them was Christa McAuliffe, a schoolteacher from New Hampshire, who had won a nationwide competition to fly in the shuttle. A set of faulty gaskets joining rocket-booster sections have been blamed for the disaster.

A LOOK AT
FASHION
IN THE '80s

The 1980s was a decade when people liked to show off their wealth, and one way of doing so was to wear expensive clothes. One of the most significant fashion trends of the first half of the 1980s was "power dressing." Clothes worn by power dressers—who included both men and women—were very sharp and were intended to impress people with the money and power of the wearer.

▷ *Shoulder pads were in, especially in women's business clothes, as part of power dressing.*

◁ *Running suits became very popular for children and adults.*

This was the decade of the "Yuppie"—a name made up from the words *Young Urban Professional*. Most Yuppies worked in the financial centers of major cities, such as New York, London, and Frankfurt, and they loved to wear expensive clothes. After the great financial crash of 1987 and the recession that followed, Yuppies faded from the scene.

Designer labels

Clothes made by top fashion designers became increasingly important to very large numbers of people. Previously, these clothes were worn only by a few select individuals, such as rock stars and TV celebrities. But, in the 1980s, ordinary people were prepared to pay to own clothes with the label of a famous designer. Many designers and manufacturers made fortunes by supplying the public's taste for clothes with fashionable designer labels.

Good–bye

Bell-bottoms;
tank tops;
permed hair
for men

Hello

Shoulder pads (for
men and women);
stonewashed jeans;
running suits;
running shoes

Established fashion names, such as Ralph Lauren and Calvin Klein, were joined by those of newer designers, who included Karl Lagerfeld, Issey Miyake, and Christian Lacroix. Many of the clothes they designed for fashion shows were deliberately outrageous, and this ensured that they received a great deal of attention from the fashion press.

▷ *Among the 1980s ideas of British designer Vivienne Westwood were the mini crinoline and underwear worn as outerwear. Designer Jean Paul Gaultier took up the underwear-as-outerwear idea, and Madonna made it famous.*

...Newsflash...

Paris, June 1981. The famous Paris fashion show has been taken by storm by the new collection from a Japanese design group called "Comme des Garçons." This new wave of Japanese designers, who include Issey Miyake, Rei Kawakubo, and Yohji Yamamoto, has thrown down a challenge to Western fashion ideas. The designers refuse to use bright colors. Their collection features loose-fitting clothes produced from new materials used in exciting and unusual ways.

Top Japanese fashion designer Issey Miyake said this about his clothes:

"Without the wearer's ingenuity, my clothing isn't clothing. These are clothes where room is left for wearers to make things their own."

International fashion

The old fashion centers of Paris and Rome began to face competition from designers in Milan and New York. In many cases, these young designers forced the major fashion houses to follow current trends more closely. Inside the older fashion houses, there were a number of top designers who kept them in touch with modern fashion. They included Karl Lagerfeld at Chanel.

Italian designer Giorgio Armani, who had made a name for himself in the 1970s, became popular and very influential in the 1980s. In the 1980s, Armani began to design women's clothing that drew attention to the shape of the body, and he accentuated it with luxurious, tactile fabrics. His clothes were widely recognized and owning them became a status symbol. Many celebrities took care to be seen wearing his designs.

▷ *Armani-designed clothes modeled in Milan in 1989*

Models become stars

Just as fashion designers became household names, so too did the models who wore their clothes. The late 1980s marked the beginning of the age of the supermodel, women who were paid fortunes to wear top designer clothes. Among the new breed of supermodel were Linda Evangelista and Cindy Crawford. Their faces were seen on the covers of magazines around the world. In the 1990s many would become as famous as movie stars.

◁ *Model Christie Brinkley, with singer Billy Joel, who wrote a hit song ("Uptown Girl") about her*

Triumph of the sneaker

Another, very different trend began to emerge in the 1980s. This was based on people's interest in sports and other leisure activities. Running clothes, once used only by athletes and other sports people, now began to be worn by adults and children for everyday wear. Women carried this idea further by wearing joggers and leggings outside the gym. But the single most important item of this new fashion was the running shoe. It originated from the simple canvas shoe and rubber sneaker, but by the 1980s it had

Athlete Jackie Aiyepong explained the attraction of sneakers:

"They're the only thing the whole world can relate to. Actors, musicians, politicians, everybody has got a pair of sneakers."

People's enthusiasm for designer labels extended to the new sports-leisure world as well, so that, for example, parents had to buy their children the "right" running suit.

Advertising

Manufacturers—and companies and organizations that had nothing to do with clothes—began to realize that they could make money by putting their names on fashion goods. People were prepared to pay extra for clothes and other items bearing the name of a company with an image that was considered "cool." And when people walked around in these clothes, they gave the company some free advertising, too. The companies that were considered cool tended to be those operating in sports and leisure, which appealed to young people. Major football teams, for example, started to sell products displaying their name, such as jackets, trousers, and backpacks.

become a hi-tech piece of running equipment, using the latest materials. Companies specializing in this footwear—such as Nike and Adidas—fought one another desperately to persuade people to buy their products. During the decade, sales of running shoes soared, and in the United States average ownership of running shoes doubled.

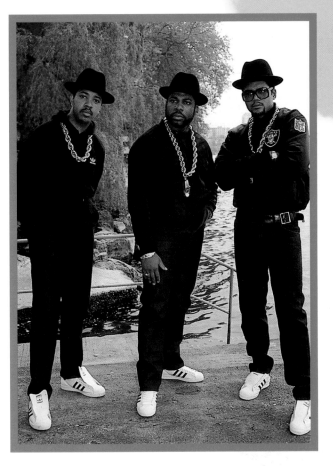

▷ At a concert in Philadelphia in 1986, rap artists Run DMC invited the audience to wave their shoes in the air while the group performed their hit, "My Adidas."

This was part of an overall trend called licensed merchandising—the manufacture and sale of a range of goods, including pens, toys, and jewelry, as well as clothes, to "tie in" with a movie, for example, or anything that was fashionable at the time.

A LOOK AT
POP MUSIC
IN THE '80s

▽ *Paul Simon (left) with South African musicians Miriam Makeba and Hugh Masekela*

Popular music in the 1980s combined influences from around the world. The great explosion of punk and new wave that had shaken music in the late 1970s died down. Many punk rock groups, such as the Sex Pistols, disbanded, and others, such as The Clash, became part of mainstream pop.

A noticeable trend in pop in the early 1980s was the emergence of the New Romantics, who wore colorful clothes and did not take their music too seriously. They included Culture Club, Adam and the Ants, and Duran Duran. Other new groups, such as Wham!, also sang about the fun side of life.

World music
A more serious type of music to emerge was world music, a combination of international musical styles. In practice, this meant using folk music from Africa, Asia, or South America and combining it with Western pop rhythms and instruments.

In 1982, rock musician Peter Gabriel organized the first WOMAD (World of Music, Arts, and

Profile

Madonna (1958–)

Her full name is Madonna Louise Ciccone, and she moved from Rochester, Minnesota, to New York to seek her fortune in the music business. Her first single, "Everybody," became a 1982 hit in dance clubs and was followed by a string of hits that made her a star around the world. Madonna was very good at judging the mood of the pop world, and she changed her image to fit whatever was happening at the moment. By the end of the decade, she had set up her own film, publishing, and recording companies.

▷ *The Irish group U2 made a great impact with their albums* The Unforgettable Fire *(1984) and* The Joshua Tree *(1987).*

Dance) festival, which brought together musicians from around the world. From then on, WOMAD became a focus for world music.

Many other Western musicians began to look around the world for inspiration. Among these was the rock star Paul Simon, who went to South Africa to work with local musicians. The result was the famous *Graceland* album, which fused African rhythms and vocal harmonies with American popular music. In a later album, *Rhythm of the Saints* (released in 1990), Simon combined the musical styles of South America with those of Africa and North America, to great effect.

At the same time, musicians from the non-Western world began to find success in the West. African dance music became fashionable in Europe, especially in France, and Youssou N'Dour (a singer from the former French colony of Senegal) became a figure in Western pop music. In the United States, groups with a Mexican background, such as Los Lobos, gained a new popularity.

Stars of the Eighties

Like every other decade, the 1980s produced a host of new and rising stars. Among the brightest were Madonna, Bruce Springsteen, Bon Jovi, George Michael, and Prince. The top groups included The Police and U2.

▽ *Prince's 1982 album,* 1999, *was followed by two,* Purple Rain *and* Parade *made with his band The Revolution, and in 1987 by a solo album,* Sign O' the Times.

Madonna believed in keeping control:

"It's a great feeling to be powerful. I've been striving for it all my life. I think that's just the quest of every human being: power."

△ *Lionel Ritchie fronts the lineup of rock stars taking part in the Live Aid concert in Philadelphia in July 1985.*

Michael Jackson confirmed his international status with the release of his *Thriller* album in 1982. Two years after its release, *Thriller* had produced seven top ten singles in the United States, and after selling 25 million copies worldwide, it became the best-selling LP of all time. Jackson was famous for his long and elaborate videos, which normally featured one of his brilliant dance routines. He lived in a

vast mansion, with exotic animals, and seemed to prefer the company of children to adults. His colorful clothes and eccentric way of living continued to fascinate a global audience well into the 1990s.

Live Aid

The musical event of the decade was the holding of two charity concerts, called Live Aid, in July 1985. One concert was held in London at the same time as the other was held in Philadelphia, Pennsylvania. Both were televised live.

The inspiration for these charity concerts was the terrible 1984 famine in Ethiopia. Irish rock musician Bob Geldof (singer with the punk rock group the Boomtown Rats) was so moved by the plight of the starving people in Africa that he first persuaded a group of fellow musicians to produce a single called "Do They Know It's Christmas?" Sales of this record raised millions for famine relief at the end of 1984. This was

66 99

The heartfelt lyrics of "Do They Know It's Christmas?" included this chorus:

"Feed the world. Let them know it's Christmas."

▷ *Mark Knopfler (right) and John Ilsley of Dire Straits, one of the top groups of the 1980s*

followed by an American single—"We Are the World," written by Michael Jackson and Lionel Ritchie—and the Live Aid concerts. Thanks to a bigger satellite linkup than had ever been used before, the concerts were seen on television by an amazing 1.8 billion people around the globe. About $50 million was raised for famine relief by record and concert sales and from donations sent in by the public. In helping the starving poor in Africa, the Live Aid concerts showed that the rich (and sometimes spoiled) rock music world really did think about other people. The concerts also acted as a showcase for top rock music acts, giving them worldwide coverage.

△ *Former Beatle John Lennon lived in New York with his wife, Yoko Ono. This photograph of him (left) signing an autograph became famous because the fan in the picture, Mark Chapman, shot and killed Lennon in December 1980.*

...Newsflash...

Brooklyn, New York, July 1983. Multimedia artist Laurie Anderson is in town to perform her six-hour work called *United States, Parts I–IV.* The piece contains a mix of music, words, cartoons, and film clips. Anderson achieved stardom recently with her hit single "O Superman." She combines art, music, and drama to make a special event for her audience. Anderson is one of several performance artists who tries to use pop music to make us think differently about the world around us.

Innovations

Rock musicians in the 1980s were helped by the introduction of the 24-hour cable music channel called MTV (Music Television). Now top rock and pop acts could have their music videos broadcast around the world, from Brazil to Japan. In the world of pop, it was increasingly important to gain a worldwide audience; being big in your own country was not enough. The growth of MTV made the production of videos vitally important. More than ever, groups and singers needed to have a strong visual appeal.

Compact discs (CDs) were another innovation that came to the aid of many musicians. CDs improved the sound for the listener. Also, since many music enthusiasts bought CDs to replace the vinyl records they had bought in the 1960s and

1970s, old rock acts from the previous 20 years or so did very well, because their recordings were released for the second time.

With personal cassette players, invented in 1979, people could listen to music on their own while they were on the move. Over the decade, the Sony Walkman changed the way people listened to music.

The growth of hip-hop

The most significant musical style to emerge in the 1980s was hip-hop, which was a development from Afro-American rap music.

▷ Break dancing became a craze of the 1980s, with the dancers spinning on their heads, backs, and hands, in an amazingly acrobatic way.

A famous line from the rap song "The Message" by Grandmaster Flash describes the terrible feelings caused by poverty and drug addiction:

"Don't push me, 'cos I'm close to the edge."

The 1982 single "The Message," by Grandmaster Flash and the Furious Five, was a highly influential rap record, which explained the problems of poverty, violence, racism, and drugs that blighted people's lives in America's inner cities.

By the mid-1980s, hip-hop had extended the boundaries of rap (meaning "to talk") to include not only music, but also dance, fashion, and slang. A hip-hop look developed among young Afro-Americans. It featured baggy jeans,

Profile

Andrew Lloyd Webber (1948–)

The main person behind the revival of musicals in the 1980s was the classically trained musician Andrew Lloyd Webber. Working with lyricist Tim Rice, he first found fame with the "pop oratorio" *Joseph and the Amazing Technicolor Dreamcoat* (1968) and the rock opera *Jesus Christ Superstar* (1971). Other successes followed in the 1970s, but in 1982 Lloyd Webber made theater history by having three shows running simultaneously in New York and London: *Evita*, *Cats*, and *Starlight Express*. He was knighted in 1992.

baseball caps worn backward, gold jewelry, and high-top sneakers—worn unlaced. The look quickly spread around the Western world among teenagers. The 1984 album by Run-DMC—called *Run-DMC*—was a huge success. Hip-hop music moved out of the inner-city ghettos of the United States to become hugely popular worldwide.

The musical

In complete contrast to the tough world of hip-hop was the continuing success of the musical. One major hit was *Les Misérables*, which was based on the French novel about crime and punishment in revolutionary Paris. More important still was a series of musicals written by Andrew Lloyd Webber, which included *Cats* (1981),

Starlight Express (1983), and *The Phantom of the Opera* (1986). Although many music critics sneered at Lloyd Webber, his tunes proved immensely popular in Europe and the United States, and his shows were regular sellouts.

▽ *A duet from* The Phantom of the Opera

A LOOK AT
ART and ARCHITECTURE
IN THE '80s

The art world benefited from the 1980s financial boom. Rich people used their spare money to buy works of art. This was especially true in the United States. New York City's SoHo district was the center of the enthusiasm for modern art.

Among the many American artists who established international reputations in the 1980s was Julian Schnabel. One of his trademark styles was to stick pieces of broken crockery onto his paintings. Another successful artist was Jeff Koons, who produced life-size statues of the singer Michael Jackson and a giant "inflatable" rabbit made from stainless steel. Even more extreme was Jenny Holzer, whose artwork consisted of messages written on T-shirts, postcards, and electronic message boards. One such message, displayed in New York City's Times Square, read simply: "Money Creates Taste."

▽ Jeff Koons's stainless steel rabbit, 1986, is more than 3 ft. (1 m) high.

Art in the subway

An artistic development that also came mainly from New York was graffiti art. Its origins went back to the elaborately drawn words and slogans that were sprayed onto New York subway trains as an act of vandalism. Bright colors and big letters were an essential part of this graffiti. In time, graffiti artists moved from the subway and began to cover other large surfaces in the inner city. There, the painting caught the imagination of other artists and gallery owners. Soon, graffiti artists, such as Jean-Michel Basquiat, were exhibiting their work in fashionable galleries.

Another artist who began in graffiti was Keith Haring, who used chalk to create distinctive squiggly line drawings on subway station walls. During the 1980s his work became immensely popular, and in 1986 he opened his own store in SoHo. Although his artwork could cost many thousands of dollars, he used his store—called Haring's Pop Shop—

to sell cheap items, such as decorated T-shirts and badges, for as little as $10. An active campaigner for AIDS charities, Haring died of the disease in 1990.

◁ *Self-portrait of a graffiti artist*

Strange materials

Conceptual art was popular in the 1980s and involved artists spending time and thought in imagining the "idea" behind the work of art. Leading conceptual artists included Joseph Beuys, a German, who brought many strange materials together. A famous series of exhibits he produced used just lard and felt.

...Newsflash...

New York, November 11, 1987. Vincent van Gogh's painting *Irises* was bought today by Australian tycoon Alan Bond for $53.9 million. Prices for major works of art have been rising steeply throughout the decade. The works are thought to be a good investment in times of economic turmoil. Van Gogh painted *Irises* in an asylum in 1889 and was unable to sell the picture in his own lifetime. The last time this painting came up for sale was in 1947, when it raised $100,000.

Christo was a Bulgarian-born artist who moved to the United States and specialized in huge works of conceptual art. In 1983 he produced a work called *Surrounded Islands*, near Miami, Florida. It involved encircling eleven small islands with enormous pink plastic aprons. Later in the decade, Christo supervised the "wrapping" of the Pont Neuf bridge in Paris (1985).

To many people, Christo seemed very odd, but he claimed that he was trying to make people see objects in a fresh way.

▽ *It took Christo nine years to negotiate permission to wrap the Pont Neuf and to plan all the work involved.*

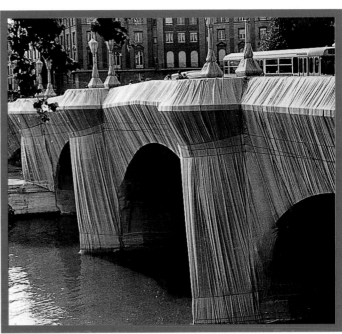

Keith Haring said that painting should be done quickly and without worrying over every little detail. He wrote:

"Graffiti art is an instant gesture. And because I'm capturing that instant, I do not believe in mistakes."

Profile

Richard Rogers (1933–)

Born of Anglo-Italian parents, Rogers studied architecture in Italy. He believed that modern architecture must not be afraid to make use of the latest technology. After working with Renzo Piano on the Pompidou Center in Paris, he was responsible for designing the Lloyd's Headquarters building in London, which opened in 1986. In both buildings, service elevators and air-conditioning ducts were not hidden; instead, they were made a feature of the design, using bright colors and transparent materials. As well as designing buildings, Rogers lectured in architecture.

New buildings

The architectural world enjoyed a golden period during the 1980s, helped by the financial boom of the first half of the decade. Not surprisingly, some of the major buildings were built for financial institutions. Two of the most famous were the Lloyd's Headquarters in London, designed by Richard Rogers, and Norman Foster's Hong Kong and Shanghai Bank in Hong Kong.

A major building program was launched in Paris by the French president, François

A famous comment of Prince Charles's on the modern design for an extension to London's National Gallery was that it was like:

"a monstrous carbuncle on the face of a much-loved and elegant friend."

▽ *The Hong Kong and Shanghai Bank, opened in 1986*

◁ La Grande Arche, Paris

Most of the great buildings of the 1980s were very brash and modern, and some people did not like them, saying that they did not fit in with other buildings around them. As a result, some architects worked in more traditional styles and designed buildings that looked back to the past. They deliberately used old materials such as brick and stone instead of new ones such as concrete and glass.

" "

The director of the Louvre pyramid project, Emile Biasini, answered the many critics of the design:

"In ten years ... the arguments will have been forgotten. The ... French will regard it as another one of their classics."

Mitterrand. One of the most controversial works was designed by the American architect I. M. Pei: a pyramid that took center stage in front of the great French art gallery of the Louvre. Much of the main building work in Paris was concentrated around the area known as La Défense, including the great European landmark building La Grande Arche, designed by Danish architect Johan von Spreckelsen.

A masterpiece of the decade was the Neue Staatsgalerie in Stuttgart, Germany, whose architects were James Stirling and Michael Wilford. It combined different architectural styles in one exciting structure. Other key works were Jørn Utzon's National Assembly Building in Kuwait and Frank Gehry's California Aerospace Museum in Los Angeles, California.

▽ The California Aerospace Museum

A LOOK AT
SPORTS
IN THE '80s

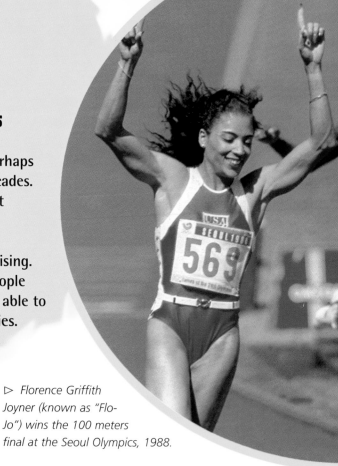

Money and politics dominated sports—perhaps more so in the 1980s than in other decades. Television companies were eager to broadcast major sports events. This would increase the numbers of viewers and thus enable the companies to make more money from advertising. The organizations running the sports that people liked to watch on TV—such as football—were able to demand high payments from the TV companies.

Politics and sports

Following the Soviet invasion of Afghanistan in 1979, the United States decided not to attend the 1980 Olympic Games that were held in Moscow.

▷ *Florence Griffith Joyner (known as "Flo-Jo") wins the 100 meters final at the Seoul Olympics, 1988.*

...Newsflash...

Seoul, South Korea, October 2, 1988. As the 1988 Olympics end, a new controversy echoes around the world. The Canadian sprinter Ben Johnson had set a new 100 meters record, with a time of just 9.79 seconds. But a subsequent drug test revealed that Johnson had taken the banned substance anabolic steroids, which gave him an unfair advantage. Johnson has been stripped of his gold medal (which will go instead to second-placed Carl Lewis of the United States) and has been banned from international competitions for two years.

Many other Western countries joined the boycott, so these Olympics were not a true competition among the best athletes in the world. Much the same thing happened at the 1984 Games in Los Angeles. This time, the Soviet Union and communist countries from Eastern Europe refused to attend.

Proper competition was restored at the 1988 Olympic Games, held in the South Korean capital of Seoul. The fact that top athletes both from the West and from communist countries had not competed for more than ten years gave these games a special interest. The women track athletes from the United States did particularly well, with the flamboyant Florence Griffith Joyner gaining gold and a world record in the 100 meter-race. Overall, however, the Soviet Union did best, with a total of 132 gold, silver, and bronze medals. But the games were overshadowed by the Ben Johnson scandal, which revealed the high levels of drug use among top sports stars.

John McEnroe often lost his temper with referees. In 1981 he shouted one of his best-known remarks to a referee:

"Man, you cannot be serious!"

Tennis

In tennis, the men's game saw some epic battles between American stars John McEnroe and Jimmy Connors. Joining them at the top were the Czech-American Ivan Lendl, Swedish player Matts Wilander, and, in the second half of the decade, the young stars Boris Becker from Germany and Stefan Edberg from Sweden.

The women's game was dominated by Martina Navratilova. Although the American Chris Evert also fought hard, it was not until 1988, with the emergence of German player Steffi Graf, that Navratilova faced any serious challenge.

Boxing highlights

One of boxing's highlights in the 1980s was the competition between the great middleweights Sugar Ray Leonard and Marvin Hagler. Leonard defeated Hagler in 1987 to win the World Middleweight Championship. Heavyweight boxing was set on fire when the tough street fighter Mike Tyson defeated Michael Spinks to win the World Championship in 1988.

△ *April 7, 1987: middleweight Sugar Ray Leonard (right) throws a punch at Marvin Hagler.*

Profile

Martina Navratilova (1956–)

Martina Navratilova dominated women's tennis in the 1980s, and also raised the women's game to new levels of power and speed. Born in Czechoslovakia, she later moved to the United States and became an American citizen in 1981. Navratilova won Wimbledon a record nine times, and by 1992, when she retired, she had won 54 Grand Slam events within a total of 158 championships—far more than any male or other female player in the history of the game.

▷ *A Williams Honda driven by Nelson Piquet, world champion in 1981, 1983, and 1987.*

Motor and cycle racing

In Formula One motor racing, the top team was McLaren, which, with Porsche, and then Honda engines, won five world championships. The runner-up team was Williams, with three world championships. The best drivers were the Brazilian Nelson Piquet and the Frenchman Alain Prost, with three world championships each, although one of the rising stars of the decade was the young Brazilian Ayrton Senna.

Cycling became an increasingly professional sport, with teams from Europe and the United States competing for the major honors. The Tour de France remained the ultimate test of a cyclist's strength, skill, and courage. The course was 3,000 miles (5,000 km) long, much of it over high mountains. One of the more surprising developments was the breakthrough of American cyclist Greg LeMond. He won the

Tour in 1986, 1989, and then again in 1990, making him one of cycling's greatest stars.

Basketball and football

Basketball, a dominant sport in the United States, became increasingly popular in Europe. Basketball leagues with professional players became established in many European countries. Much of the new international

Profile

"Magic" Johnson (1959–)

Earvin "Magic" Johnson became a major basketball star, playing for the Los Angeles' Lakers team. He earned his nickname for the brilliance of his playing style, which seemed almost magical. During the 1980s he became the most valuable player in the game.

In 1991, however, he retired from basketball after he found out that he was HIV positive (a series of symptoms that could develop into AIDS). He then went on to campaign about the dangers of HIV and AIDS, and to encourage young people to take up sports.

Profile

Michael Laudrup (1964–)

This highly talented Danish soccer player (on the right) began his career with the local team Brondbyernes. Then he was signed up by the giant Italian club Juventus, where he was involved in winning the World Club Cup in 1985. He later moved to Spain and played first for Barcelona—winning the 1989 European Cup Winners' Cup—and then for Real Madrid. Laudrup was typical of many young players of the time, who moved around Europe, playing for the best clubs that could afford them. In 1986 he played for Denmark in the World Cup.

interest in basketball was a result of the attention attracted by top players such as Michael Jordan and "Magic" Johnson. These stars earned vast amounts of money by endorsing sportswear products.

But the most popular game in many parts of the world was still soccer, played by millions of people and watched by billions! The 1982 World Cup held in Spain was won by Italy. The next World Cup (Mexico, 1986) was won by an Argentinian team, led by the brilliant but unstable Diego Maradona. During a match against England, Maradona knocked the ball into the net, using his hand. Although this was deliberate cheating—he called it

▷ Argentinian football captain Diego Maradona shows off the World Cup trophy at the end of the final against Germany, 1986.

the "hand of God"—there could be no doubt that Maradona was the best soccer player in the world at that time.

Soccer in England—the country that invented the modern game—went through a bad period in the 1980s. Crowd trouble was a particular problem, with gangs of so-called supporters from one club attacking the supporters from another. In 1985, British hooligans were responsible for the deaths of 39 supporters at a European game at Heysel in Belgium. In 1989, an even worse event took place at the Hillsborough stadium in Sheffield in England, when 95 people were crushed to death because of overcrowding and poor policing. As a result of these incidents, soccer stadiums and the organization of supporters were improved.

A LOOK AT
LEISURE and ENTERTAINMENT
IN THE '80s

The leisure and entertainment industries became bigger and more powerful during the 1980s. People throughout the Western world spent billions of dollars for their own pleasure and amusement.

Television

The biggest single form of entertainment was television, and during the 1980s it was transformed by new channels and by new ways of broadcasting. The CNN news channel was started in 1980, broadcasting only news via satellite or cable. Few people at the time thought that CNN would succeed, but by the end of the decade its news stories were being transmitted throughout the world.

Another key global success story was MTV (Music Television), which was set up in 1981. MTV was designed not only for viewers in the United States but also for an international audience interested in pop music. Although it only transmitted music videos, it had a great influence on pop music itself, helping launch the careers of singers such as Michael Jackson and Madonna.

The new TV channels did not rely on the old

◁ Aaron Spelling's TV series Dynasty was the story of business tycoon, Blake Carrington (John Forsythe) his wife, Krystle (Linda Evans), and—the power-dressed villain—his ex-wife, Alexis Colby (Joan Collins).

national and "terrestrial" broadcasting systems, but used either satellite or cable. This was the beginning of a broadcasting revolution that would continue well into the 1990s.

◁ *A new way of making home movies arrived with the camcorder. During the decade, TV programs were made from humorous clips sent in by viewers from their own home videos.*

TV shows of the decade

The TV programs that captured an international audience came mainly from the United States. *Dallas* was a drama that was based around a wealthy Texas oil family. The main character was the ruthless J. R. Ewing. When he was mysteriously shot and wounded, during an episode in 1980, television ratings around the world broke new records. At its peak, *Dallas* was broadcast in 91 countries.

Dallas was about wealth, greed, and weakness. Producer Philip Capice said:

"Viewers love to see rich people more screwed up than they are. It makes them feel superior."

TV comedy also proved popular, including shows such as *Cheers*—about a bar in Boston —and *Roseanne*, the story of a blue-collar family in the Midwest.

One other type of program that became important was the confessional talk show, where a host encouraged people to talk about problems in their lives. Host Oprah Winfrey became famous for the way she identified with the people on her show.

Profile

Oprah Winfrey (1954–)

Oprah Winfrey entered television in the 1980s with a local talk show based in Chicago. It was successful because she made her guests feel at home, especially as they talked about difficult problems such as homelessness and sexual abuse. Oprah was also prepared to talk about her own difficulties, including problems with her weight and with close relationships. In 1986 her show was broadcast nationally and became a ratings winner all over the United States. Oprah has been in several Hollywood movies and was Oscar-nominated for her role in *The Color Purple*.

Film director Steven Spielberg said that his early life was influenced by:

"growing up with three parents— a mother, a father, and a TV set."

◁ *In Steven Spielberg's 1982 movie ET, The Extra-Terrestrial, ET becomes friends with a young American boy, Elliott.*

the *Die Hard* series, starring Bruce Willis. Less violent but equally popular was *Back to the Future*, starring Michael J. Fox as someone who goes backward and forward in time.

The development of computer animation enabled filmmakers to produce ever-better special effects to amaze their audiences.

At the movies

Big Hollywood movies attracted huge audiences around the world. Steven Spielberg made some spectacularly successful films, such as *Raiders of the Lost Ark* and *ET*. Although he used many brilliant special effects, his real achievement lay in his ability to tell a simple story very well.

Ex-bodybuilder Arnold Schwarzenegger was the star of *The Terminator*, in which he played a cyborg assassin from the future. The film was a big hit and was followed by a sequel. The *Terminator* films also influenced other Hollywood films, such as

▽ *Science fiction and action films relied on the skills of special effects experts. In one film—*Who Framed Roger Rabbit?*—the human actor even costarred with a three-dimensional computer-animated rabbit!*

...Newsflash...

Milwaukee, Wisconsin, August 21, 1983. A group of computer hackers, aged 17 to 22, have broken into 20 of the country's major computer systems. Among the systems entered by the hackers was the top-secret nuclear research center at the Los Alamos National Laboratory. Reports that other computer hackers have broken into different sites around the United States, including the Pentagon, have raised new fears about computer security.

As people bought video recorders (VCRs) to tape TV programs, a new leisure industry started, that of renting movies on video for people to watch at home.

▷ *Virtual Reality machines began to be installed in amusement arcades. Wearing the special helmet, users were able to interact with a three-dimensional world that seemed almost real.*

66 99

Computer expert Jaron Lanier was a pioneer of the computer-generated 3-D world he called Virtual Reality:

"It's the first place that exists between people like the physical world, except that it's totally under our control, unlike the physical world."

Computers for play

The electronic revolution also changed people's leisure activities. Personal computers (PCs) had been intended for business use, but much of their popularity resulted from people using them to play computer games. These games became increasingly complex as the decade went on. The obsessional interest in computers shown by some young people became a concern in the 1980s. Parents tried to limit the time their children spent with their computers.

As well as games for PCs, the 1980s saw the development of console computer systems and games. Originally, these had been confined to large amusement arcade machines, but in the 1980s they moved into the home. The Pac-Man game of 1981 was a major advance in game technology, but the real breakthrough came with the Nintendo's Game Boy system in 1985.

The success of the CD as a means of storing information led to the development of the CD-ROM at the end of the decade. This was the beginning of the multimedia revolution, which would continue in the 1990s.

Getting fit

Although people were spending much time sitting down watching television or looking at computer screens, there was a growing movement toward taking part in sports and other healthy activities.

Rollerskating provided the origin for skateboarding, which developed into a major international craze in the 1980s. Another sport that made use of things from other activities was windsurfing, combining a surfboard and a dinghy sail.

Mountain biking began in California, when young people started cycling down hilly trails. Soon, special bikes were being built with extra gears, stronger frames, and wide tires to cope with rough terrain.

△ *Windsurfing was one of the great success stories among the new activity sports of the 1980s. Rather than just being a craze, it remained popular around the world.*

Activities such as mountain biking and windsurfing became more than just sports, as people who took part in them wore special clothes and developed their own special languages.

Profile

Jane Fonda (1937–)

Film star and political activist, campaigning for peace and a better environment, Jane Fonda attracted international attention in 1981 when she published *Jane Fonda's Workout Book*. The book, which encouraged women to improve their diets and exercise, was followed by music cassettes, a video—the top-seller of all time— and the setting up of exercise studios. Women worldwide followed Fonda's advice to get fit, and a new exercise industry was born. During the 1980s she continued to act. Films she appeared in include *On Golden Pond* and *The Morning After*.

Marathons and more

The new interest in healthy living reached an extreme with the development of marathons, which were held in major cities around the world. The idea behind marathons, which originated in New York City, was to develop a race that would allow ordinary people to compete with recognized long-distance runners. The London Marathon, for example, attracted up to 20,000 runners, many of whom had never done much physical activity before. Many people were sponsored to run for charity, and some did it in fancy dress.

> ▷ *April 1988: a sea of marathon runners make their way toward Boston, Massachusetts, just after the start of the Boston Marathon in Hopkinton.*

More restrained than running 26-mile marathons, but attracting even more people, was the growing interest in aerobics. Jane Fonda made aerobics popular throughout the world, especially among women. They found aerobics a useful and a social way of keeping in shape.

Shop till you drop

Shopping was nothing new, but during the 1980s it virtually became a new leisure activity. The development of big, enclosed shopping malls, complete with fast-food outlets, and vast out-of-town superstores changed the way in which people bought things. Going shopping became a "day out" for many people.

Hello
Adventure vacations; *Indiana Jones*; Computer nerds; Super Mario Brothers; Sonic the Hedgehog; McDonald's— around the world

The world of leisure and entertainment grew ever more complex and expensive. The manufacturers of electrical goods— including personal computers, VCRs, and the Sony Walkman— made fortunes because people were determined to enjoy themselves, no matter what the cost.

Date List

1980

April 18▷ The former white-dominated African colony of Rhodesia is renamed Zimbabwe. A black majority government under Robert Mugabe comes to power after full democratic elections.

May 19▷ Eight people are killed when Mount St. Helens volcano erupts in Washington state. Dust thrown up by the volcano spreads around the world, affecting the global climate.

September 30▷ Led by Saddam Hussein, Iraq invades Iran to capture the oil-rich province of Khuzistan. Eight years of bitter warfare begin.

November 4▷ Former Hollywood actor Ronald Reagan is elected president.

December 8▷ John Lennon, former coleader of the Beatles, is shot dead by a fanatic outside Lennon's New York City home.

1981

January 20▷ 52 U.S. hostages, held captive by the Iranians for 444 days, are finally released and will fly home to the United States.

July 29▷ Prince Charles, heir to the British throne, marries Lady Diana Spencer.

October 6▷ Egyptian leader President Anwar el-Sadat is assassinated by Islamic militants, angry at Sadat's peace treaty with Israel.

December 17▷ Continuing strikes in Poland lead the government to introduce martial law.

1982

April 2▷ Argentinian forces invade the Falkland Islands, and this leads to war with Great Britain. The British recapture the islands in June and force the Argentinians to surrender.

July 16▷ The Reverend Sun Myung Moon marries 2,075 couples from his Unification Church at a mass wedding ceremony in New York City.

September 18▷ Right-wing Lebanese Christian forces murder Palestinian refugees in the Sabra and Chatila camps outside Beirut. The Israeli government is condemned for allowing the massacres to take place.

October 29▷ In Spain's first democratic elections since the 1930s, a left-wing government is elected, with Felipe Gonzalez as leader.

1983

May 11▷ A German journalist admits that he forged the recently published diaries of the German dictator Adolf Hitler.

June 24▷ The space shuttle *Challenger* returns to base after a mission with astronaut Sally Ride, the first American woman to go into space.

October 23▷ A Muslim terrorist drives a truck full of explosives into the American Embassy in Beirut, killing 216 people. Another explosion kills 58 in a compound used by French peacekeeping forces.

October 31▷ U.S. troops invade the small Caribbean island of Grenada and overthrow the Marxist government that had taken control.

1984

23 April▷ French and U.S. researchers independently announce the discovery of a new virus, which they think is the cause of AIDS.

31 October▷ Indian Prime Minister Indira Gandhi is murdered by two of her bodyguards, Sikh extremists who accuse the government of discriminating against people of the Sikh religion.

December 10▷ South African civil rights activist Bishop Desmond Tutu is awarded the Nobel Peace Prize. He believes in nonviolent protest against apartheid in South Africa.

1985

March 13 ▷ After the death of Konstantin Chernenko, leadership of the Soviet Union passes to Mikhail Gorbachev.

September 1 ▷ French and U.S. researchers report finding the hulk of the *Titanic* in the mid-Atlantic, 73 years after the ship was sunk.

October 7 ▷ Palestinian terrorists take over the passenger ship *Achille Lauro*, on a cruise in the Mediterranean. One American passenger is killed before the hostages are released.

November 21 ▷ Ronald Reagan and Mikhail Gorbachev meet for the first time in Geneva. They discuss nuclear arms control.

1986

January 31 ▷ Seven astronauts are killed when the space shuttle *Challenger* explodes shortly after takeoff.

February 28 ▷ Swedish Prime Minister Olaf Palme is killed by an unknown assassin while walking through the streets of Stockholm.

April 21 ▷ U.S. aircraft bomb targets in Libya. According to U.S. officials, this is "punishment" for Libya's alleged encouragement of terrorism.

November ▷ Spilling of chemicals into the Rhine near its source in Switzerland is causing severe environmental damage throughout the river.

December 30 ▷ President Reagan acknowledges that "mistakes were made" in the illegal supply of money and arms to right-wing "Contra" rebels in Nicaragua.

1987

May 30 ▷ West German teenage pilot Matthias Rust lands a light aircraft in Moscow's Red Square. Russian air-defense officials are highly embarrassed by this publicity stunt.

October 20 ▷ The world economy is shaken by the collapse of the Wall Street Market.

December 10 ▷ The United States and the Soviet Union sign a historic treaty to limit the size of their nuclear arsenals.

1988

May 16 ▷ Some Soviet troops leave Afghanistan, the opening stage of a planned withdrawal. The Soviet Army fought the U.S.-backed Afghan rebels for eight years but was unable to defeat them.

September 19 ▷ The Burmese Army takes over the country, ousting a new civilian government that had promised democratic freedoms.

November 8 ▷ Republican candidate George Bush defeats his Democrat opponent Michael Dukakis to become the next president. Bush will succeed Ronald Reagan.

December 2 ▷ Benazir Bhutto becomes prime minister of Pakistan, the first woman to head a modern Muslim state.

1989

February 24 ▷ The Iranian government declares the writer Salman Rushdie's book *The Satanic Verses* to be blasphemous. They sentence him to death and issue a reward for his murder.

March 30 ▷ The oil-tanker *Exxon Valdez* runs aground off Alaska, spilling millions of barrels of crude oil over the coastline. Millions of fish and seabirds are killed.

June 5 ▷ Units of the Chinese Army crush the Chinese democracy movement. Student demonstrators claim that as many as 2,000 people have been killed by the army.

November 10 ▷ The Berlin Wall, which divided the city into two halves, is pulled down by demonstrators. This is a key event in the downfall of the East German communist state and a first step toward German reunification.

Glossary

apartheid

A political system in South Africa based on racial segregation, where a white government ruled over a black majority. The system ended in 1992.

blue collar

An expression used for working-class people—especially in the United States—because of the blue shirts worn by many factory workers.

boycott

To refuse to take part or have anything to do with a product, organization, or event.

cable TV

Similar to satellite TV in that many channels can be broadcast, but, instead of using a satellite, the TV signal is transmitted to the customer's TV set using underground cables.

CD

Compact Disc: a small disc that can hold audio (sound) signals in a digital format—usually music—that can then be played back, using a CD player. Generally superior to the older systems using vinyl records.

CD-ROM

Compact Disc Read Only Memory: similar in appearance to a CD, the CD-ROM is used in computers to provide large amounts of information including text, sound, and pictures.

CFC

Chlorofluorocarbon, a chemical compound used in products such as aerosols and refrigerators. Found to be harmful to the environment, CFCs have been banned by most countries.

Cold War

A period of tension from the late 1940s to the end of the 1980s, between the Soviet Union (and its allies) and the United States and other Western states. Neither side wished to fight an all-out war, so the conflict was limited to relatively minor "cold" operations such as spying.

communism

A political and economic system where the government (or state) has total control of industry and agriculture. The Soviet Union was the first country to adopt communism, setting up a one-party system that prohibited all opposition.

conceptual art

A type of art in which the idea, or concept, is as important as the content of the work.

Contras

Right-wing guerrillas, supported by the United States, who fought against the left-wing government in Nicaragua.

corrupt

Using a position of power in a dishonest way, and open to bribery.

democratic

A democratic society is one in which all adults are able to vote in elections and have a say in the way the government is run.

endorse

To show approval of a product, by allowing one's name to be used in advertisements for it. Celebrities are given money for endorsing products.

entrepreneurs

Businesspeople who take the risk of investing money in the development of a new product or in the setting up of a company. They believe they will make more money eventually when the product or company succeeds.

ghetto

An area of a city in which poor people live, especially those from ethnic minorities.

graffiti

Words and pictures that are painted or sprayed on walls and buildings. Although usually illegal, some graffiti is of a very high standard, and some people consider it to be a special art form.

hackers

People who try to break into other computer systems. Usually very skilled in using computers, they often carry out hacking just for fun.

Hezbollah

An extreme Islamic fundamentalist organization whose name means "Party of God." It was supported by the Iranian government in the 1980s and used terrorist tactics against people in Israel and the West.

Hollywood

An area of Los Angeles that is the center of the movie industry. Sometimes the word is used to describe a glitzy, spectacular event.

martial law

A system of law and order imposed over a country by its army, especially after unrest or during a breakdown in normal civilian government.

meltdown

The very dangerous condition describing the overheating of a nuclear reactor, which causes radioactive material to escape into the atmosphere.

microprocessor

One of the smallest functioning units in a computer, and one of the most important. The number (and capability) of microprocessors in a computer determines the power of the computer.

militant

A person who feels very strongly about a cause —such as a religion or animal rights—and is prepared to take action in support of it.

pesticides

Chemicals used to protect crops by killing pests such as insects. Pesticides can also kill other forms of animal and plant life that are not harmful to crops. Many environmentalists think that pesticides are used too often and too heavily.

PLO

The Palestine Liberation Organization. Originally, the PLO was a group that used terrorism to try to destroy Israel, but during the 1980s, it began to accept Israel as a proper state.

pollution

The harmful action of artificial substances, such as chemical liquids and gases, on the environment. During the 1980s there was increasing international cooperation to try to limit the damage caused by pollution.

recession

A decline of activity and output in a country's economy, causing hardship and unemployment.

republican

In Ireland, a person who believes that Northern Ireland should leave the UK and become part of the Irish Republic.

satellite TV

A new form of broadcasting that uses a satellite in space to transmit the television signal. Many more channels can be broadcast by satellite TV than by the traditional "terrestrial" system.

socialist

A supporter of socialism, a belief that the government should play a central role in the way people live and that a nation's wealth should be shared equally among its people. Socialism is similar to communism, but it is not as extreme.

stock market

A market or system in which stocks and shares in major companies are traded to the general public, using stockbrokers.

terrorism

The use of violence and intimidation to try to force a government to accept the demands of a particular group. Spectacular acts of violence are often used to draw international attention to the terrorists' cause.

The people in the picture on page 4 are
Front row, left to right:
President Reagan, United States; President Felix Boigny, Ivory Coast; Interim President Abdus Sattar, Bangladesh; President Chadli Benjedid, Algeria; Foreign Minister Hans Genscher, Germany; Prime Minister Pierre Trudeau, Canada; President Lopez Portillo, Mexico; Prince Fahd, Saudi Arabia; Foreign Minister Willibald Pahr, Austria; Foreign Minister Ramiro Guerriro, Brazil; Prime Minister Zhao Ziyang, China; President Ferdinand Marcos, Philippines.
Back row, left to right:
President Sergej Kraigher, Yugoslavia; President Julius Nyerere, Tanzania; Prime Minister Margaret Thatcher, Britain; Prime Minister Zenko Suzuki, Japan; President Forbes Burnham, Guyana; President François Mitterrand, France; Prime Minister Indira Gandhi, India; President Alhaji Shehu Shagari, Nigeria; Prime Minister Thorbiorn Falldin, Sweden; President Luis Herrera Campina, Venezuela; UN Secretary General Kurt Waldheim.

Resources

Books

Among the more accessible books on this decade are a couple of short volumes written for young readers: *The 1980s* by Richard Tames (Franklin Watts, 1990) and *We Were There in the 1980s* by Rosemary Rees (Heinemann, 1993).

For older readers, the 1980s sections of *The Chronicle of the 20th Century* (JL Publishing, 1992) and *Our Times: An Illustrated History of the 20th Century* (Turner Publishing Inc., 1995) are very informative.

Relying heavily on news photographs is *The Illustrated History of the 20th Century*, with text by Rupert Matthews (Ted Smart, 1993).

Several novels summed up the greediness of many people during the 1980s. They include Jay McInerney's *Bright Lights, Big City*, Tama Janowitz's *Slaves of New York*, and Bret Easton Ellis's *Less Than Zero*.

The novelist and journalist Tom Wolfe also looked at the decade with a critical eye in a book called *Bonfire of the Vanities*.

Films

In the United States, two notable films that gave a flavor of the decade were *Fatal Attraction* and *The Rain Man*.

The 1980s saw a renewed interest in the Vietnam War, and several serious films were released that examined the American role in the war. These included Oliver Stone's *Platoon* and Stanley Kubrick's *Full Metal Jacket*.

Music

The biggest event of the decade was the combined UK/U.S. Live Aid concert, which can be seen on video.

Two of the most globally influential artists of the decade were Michael Jackson and Madonna.

By comparison, the Irish group U2's album *The Joshua Tree* reflected a more serious side to popular music.

Art and architecture

Most art galleries in large towns and cities have paintings and sculpture from artists working in the 1980s. Leading artists working in this decade included Frank Auerbach, Francis Bacon, Joseph Beuys, Lucian Freud, Gilbert and George, Jenny Holzer, Jeff Koons, and Julian Schnabel.

Quotations

The quotations in this book are from: Page 4: *The Observer*, January 27, 1980; Pages 8, 23, 31, 39: *Our Times: An Illustrated History of the 20th Century*, Turner Publishing Inc., Atlanta, 1995; Page 11: *Chronicle of the 20th Century*, JL International Publishing, 1992; Page 13: Bruce Sterling, ed., *Mirrorshades*, 1986, quoted in Robert Andrews, ed., *Cassell Dictionary of Contemporary Quotations*, Cassell, 1996; Page 14: Edmund Wright, ed., *The Bloomsbury Chronological Dictionary of Quotations*, Bloomsbury, 1993; Page 17: Amanda Heggs, quoted in *The Guardian*, June 12, 1989; Page 19: Valerie Steele, *Fifty Years of Fashion*, Yale University Press, 1993; Page 21: quoted in *The Guardian*, October 23, 1998; Page 29: Ronald Tamplin, ed., *Harrap's Illustrated History of the 20th Century: The Arts*, Harrap, 1991; Page 38: James Monaco, ed., *Virgin International Encyclopedia of Film*, Virgin, 1991.

Index

© Copyright 1999 Wayland (Publishers) Ltd.